Just Puzzling!

Mazes & Dot-to-Dots

Your first stop for fun and learning!

7+

W9-AYE-486

START

Directions

Amy the Atlas
nnect the dots from **0** to **60**. Then.

20   30

Brighter Child®
An imprint of Carson-Dellosa Publishing LLC
Greensboro, North Carolina

Brighter Child®
An imprint of Carson-Dellosa Publishing LLC
P.O. Box 35665
Greensboro, NC 27425 USA

Printed in the USA • All rights reserved.   ISBN 978-1-60996-978-3
01-086121151

Table of Contents

Mazes

Bug Walk

Directions: Show the bug how to cross the leaf.

Park the Car

Directions: Drive the car to the garage.

Hammer Hunt

Directions: Help the bear find his hammer.

A Flower Garden

Directions: Help the butterfly out of the garden.

The Big Dig

Directions: Which dog will reach the buried bone?

Baby's Rattle

Directions: Help the baby crawl to her rattle.

A Cold Walk

Directions: Help the penguin find the way to its igloo.

Scott's Sled

Directions: Show Scott the trail to his sled.

Pete and Peggy Pig

Directions: Will Pete or Peggy get the ice-cream cone?

Fishy Friends

Directions: Help the striped fish swim through the coral and find its friend.

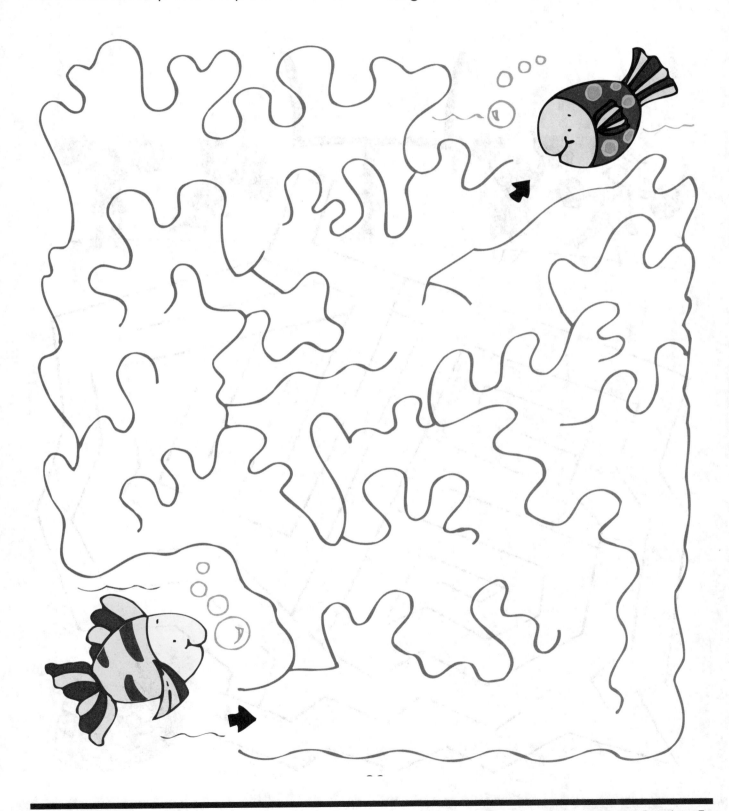

Field Goal

Directions: Kick the football through the goalposts.

All Dry

Directions: The clothes are dry. Help put them in the basket.

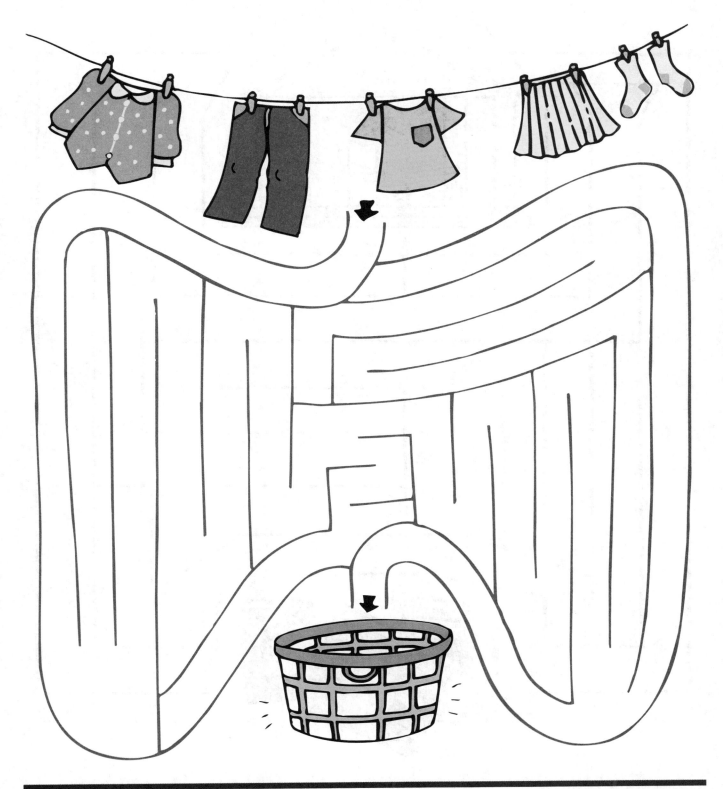

Book Return

Directions: Return the books to the library.

Time to Clean Up

Directions: Take the toys to the toy box.

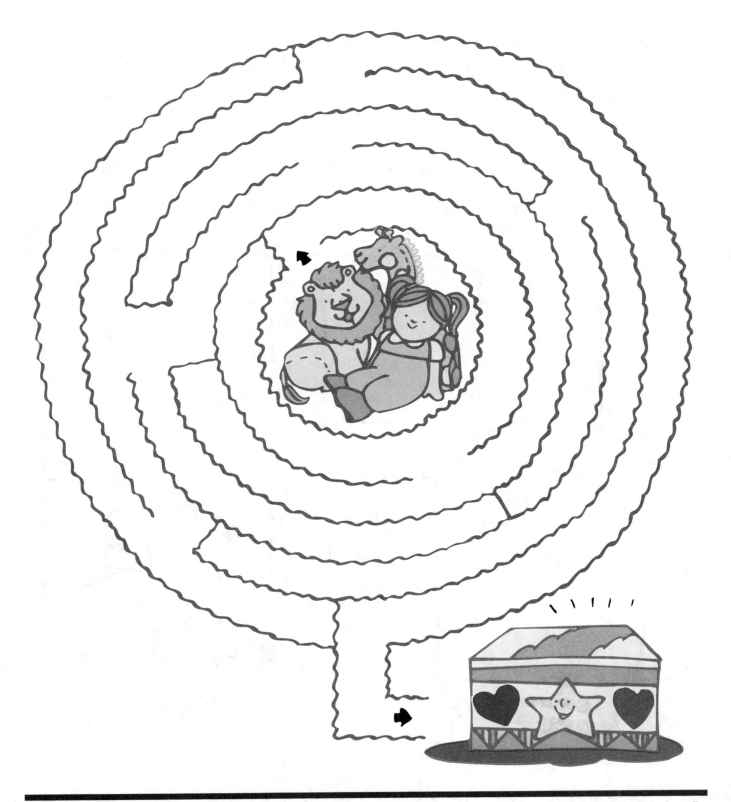

Lost Collar

Directions: Help the puppy find its collar.

Sun and Swim

Directions: Help the crocodile swim to the grassy bank.

Find the Jack-o-Lantern

Directions: Help the child get to the jack-o-lantern.

Where's Walter?

Directions: Wilma's cat Walter is missing. Help her find him.

Chef Charlie

Directions: Chef Charlie tossed the pizza crust. Where did it go?

Apple Search

Directions: Help the elephant find more apples for her pie.

Time to Rake

Directions: Help John get through the pile of leaves.

A Plate of Spaghetti

Directions: Take the fork to the bottom of the plate of pasta.

Egg Hunt

Directions: Take the bunny to the decorated egg.

Mail Delivery

Directions: Lead the pig to the mailbox.

Humpty Dumpty

Directions: Help Humpty Dumpty find the bandage. Then, color the picture.

In Space

Directions: Help the astronaut find the radio. Then, color the picture.

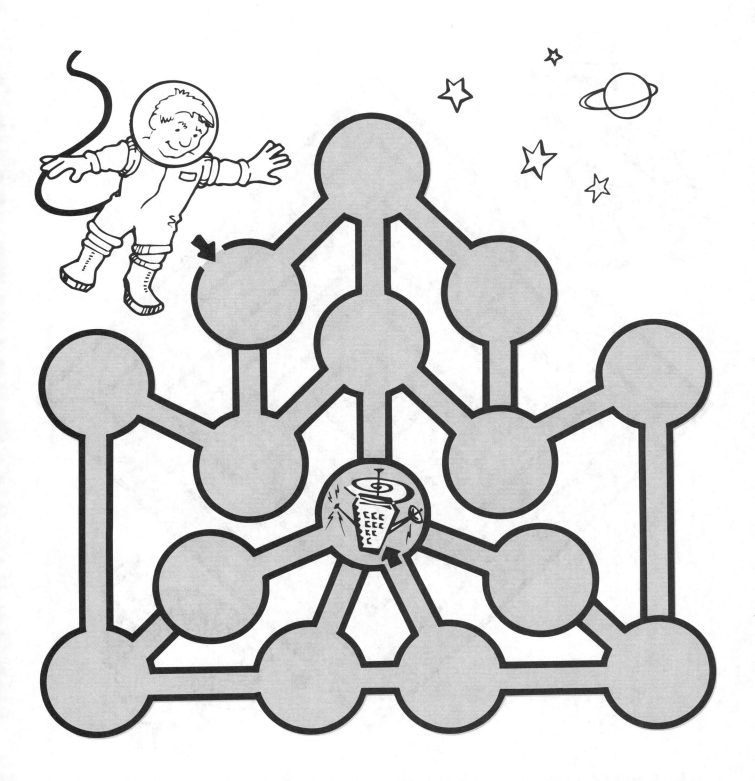

Where's the Turkey?

Directions: Help the pilgrim boy find the turkey. Then, color the picture.

Fix the Leak

Directions: Help the plumber find the sink. Then, color the picture.

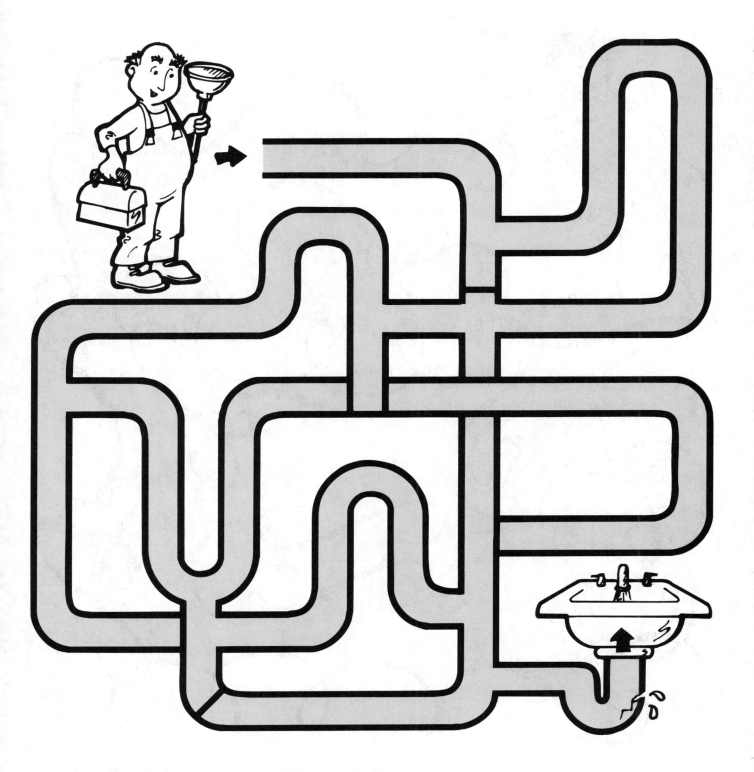

A Missing Slipper

Directions: Help the ballerina find her slipper. Then, color the picture.

A Lost Kangaroo

Directions: Help the mother kangaroo find her baby.

A Prince and a Princess

Directions: Help the prince get to the princess. Then, color the picture.

I'm Late

Directions: Help the lady get to the train. Then, color the picture.

A Perky Penguin

Directions: Help the mother penguin find the baby penguin.

Lock and Key

Directions: Help the key find the lock.

Sail Away

Directions: Help the sailor find the anchor.

Dana Deer

Directions: Connect the dots from **1** to **15**. Then, color to finish the picture.

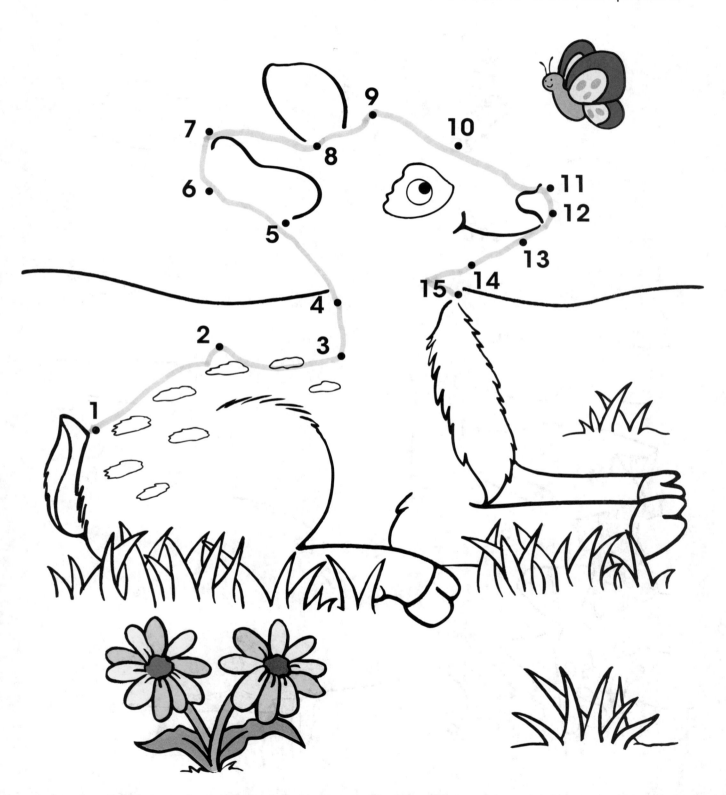

Sid Sea Lion

Directions: Connect the dots from **1** to **20**. Then, color to finish the picture.

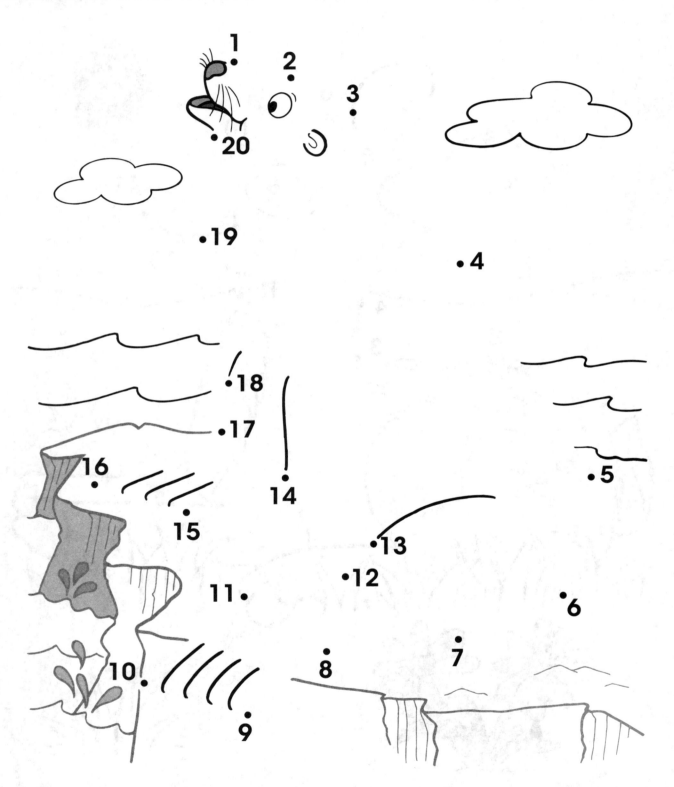

Larry Lion

Directions: Connect the dots from **1** to **25**. Then, color to finish the picture.

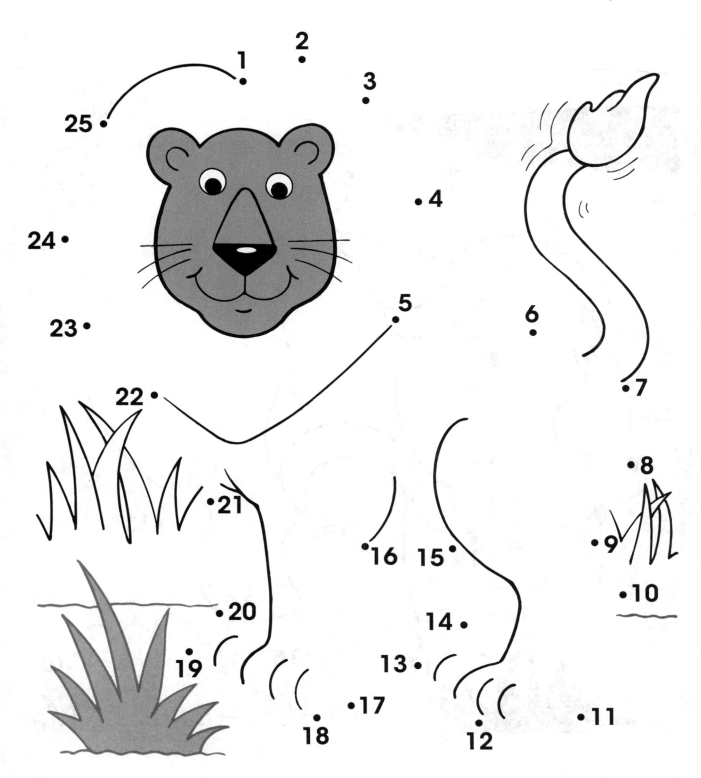

Rico Rhinoceros

Directions: Connect the dots from **1** to **25**. Then, color to finish the picture.

Patty Panda

Directions: Connect the dots from **1** to **30**. Then, color to finish the picture.

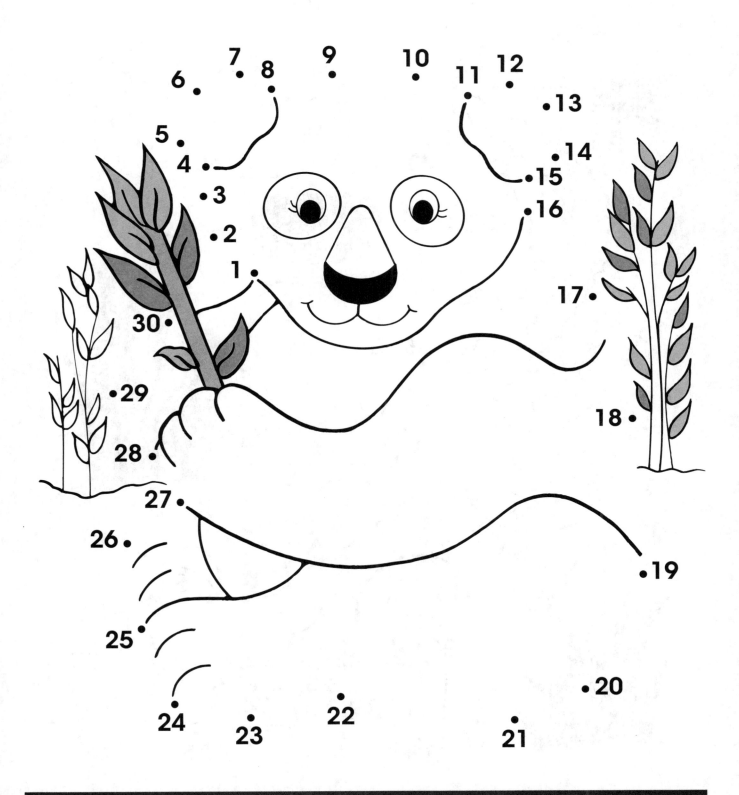

Alison Alligator

Directions: Connect the dots from **1** to **40**. Then, color to finish the picture.

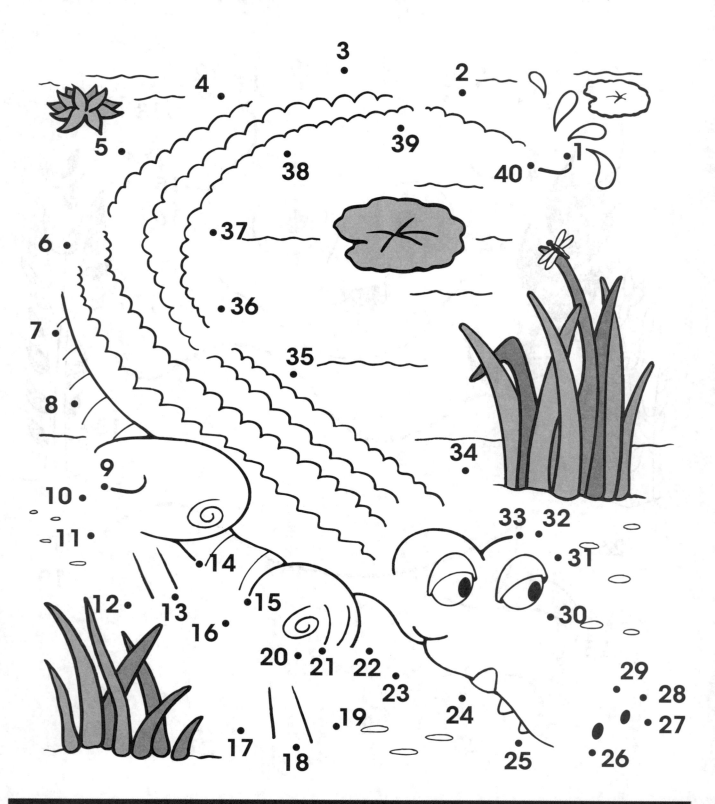

Kaori Kangaroo

Directions: Connect the dots from **1** to **50**. Then, color to finish the picture.

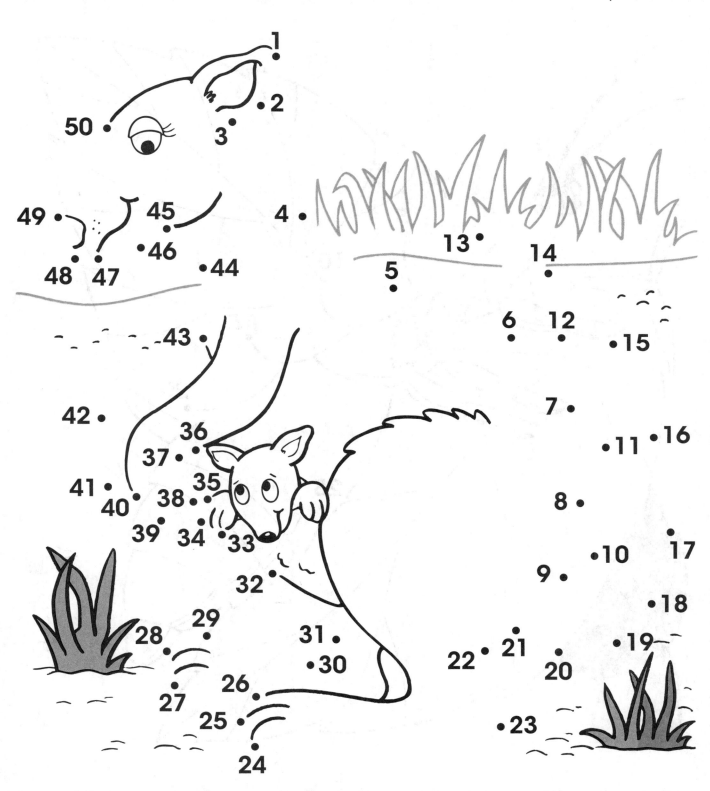

Gary the Glowworm

Directions: Connect the dots from **0** to **25**. Then, color to finish the picture.

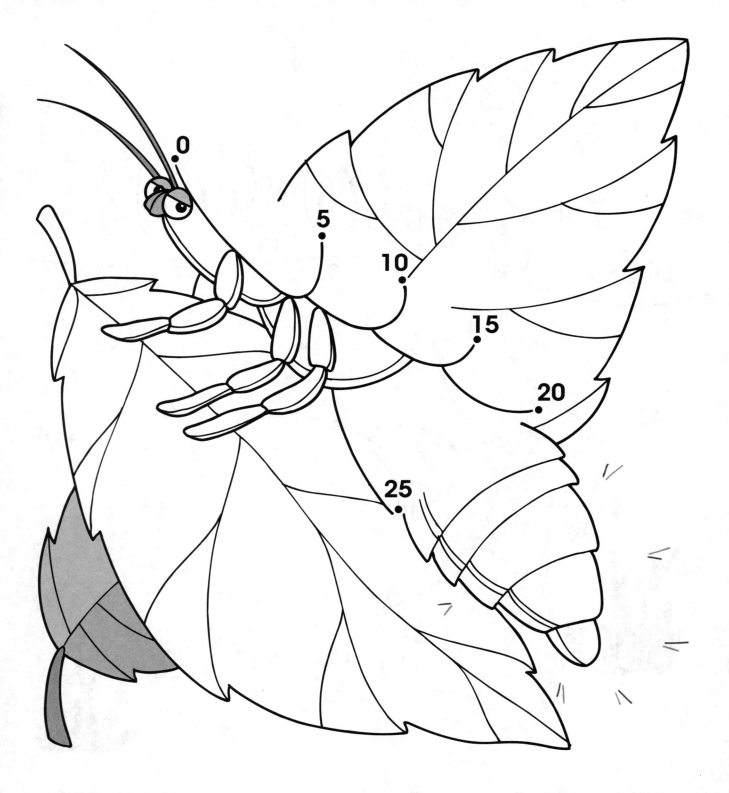

0
5
10
15
20
25

Angie the Ant

Directions: Connect the dots from **0** to **30**. Then, color to finish the picture.

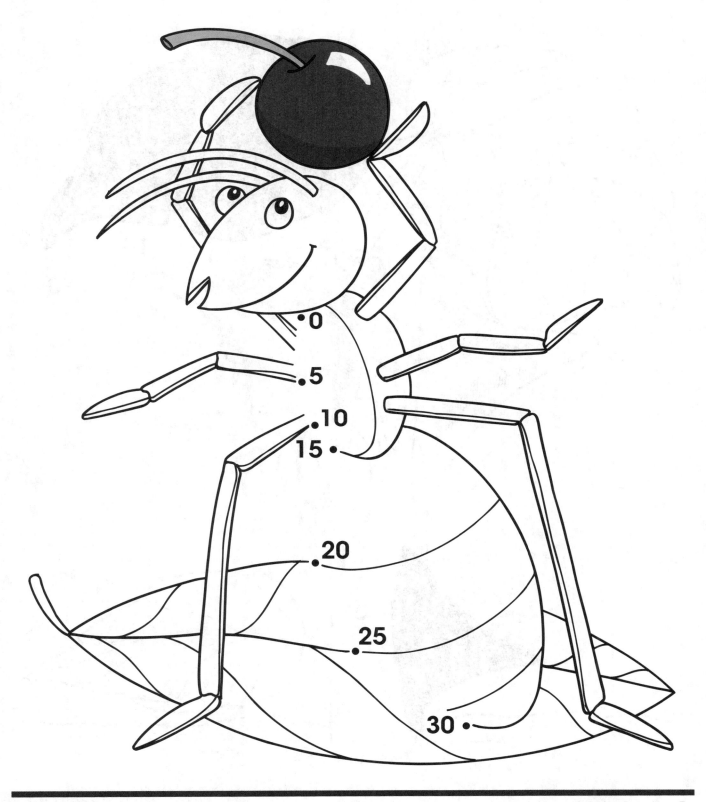

Thomas the Thorn Bug

Directions: Connect the dots from **0** to **35**. Then, color to finish the picture.

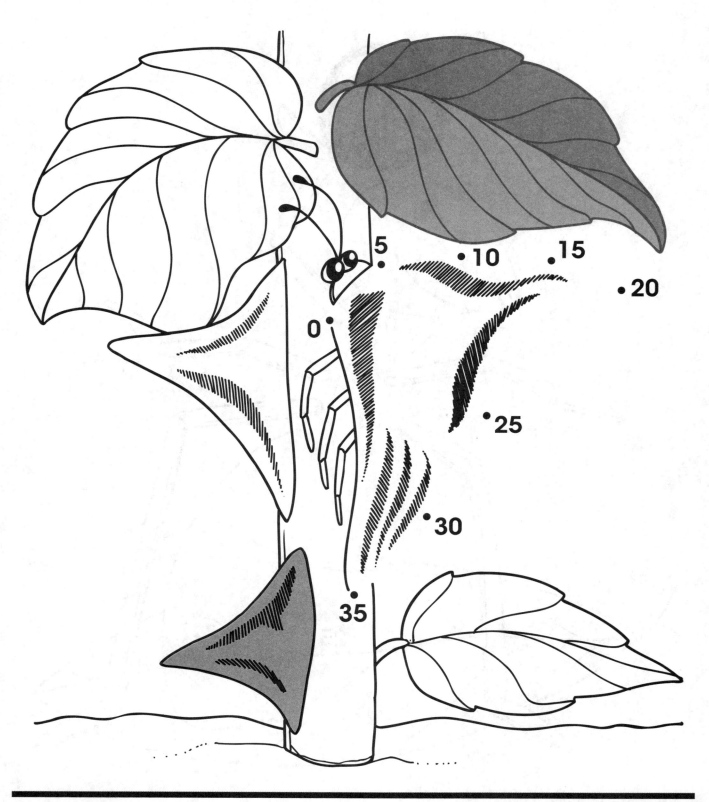

Mary the Millipede

Directions: Connect the dots from **0** to **40** Then, color to finish the picture.

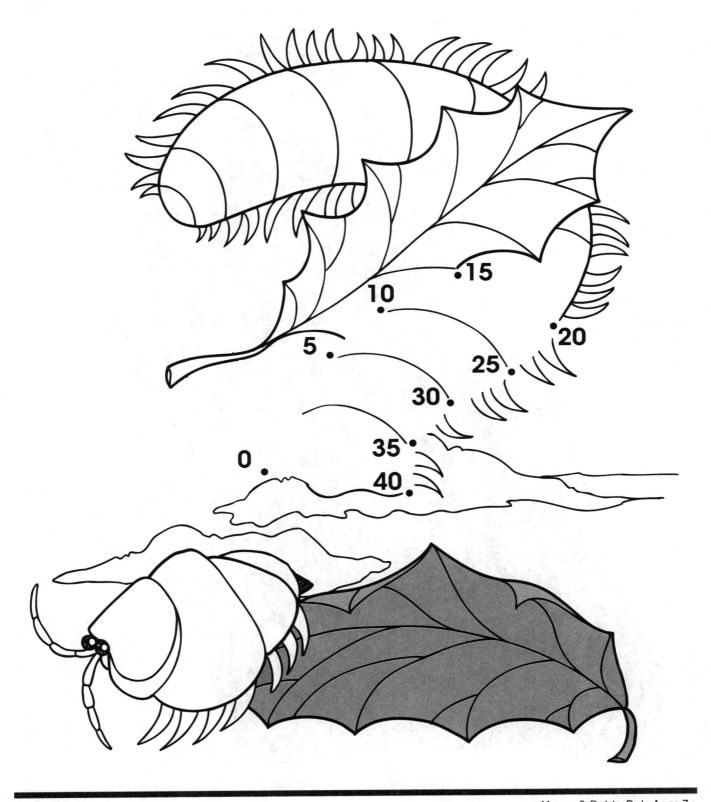

Gina the Goliath Beetle

Directions: Connect the dots from **5** to **50**. Then, color to finish the picture.

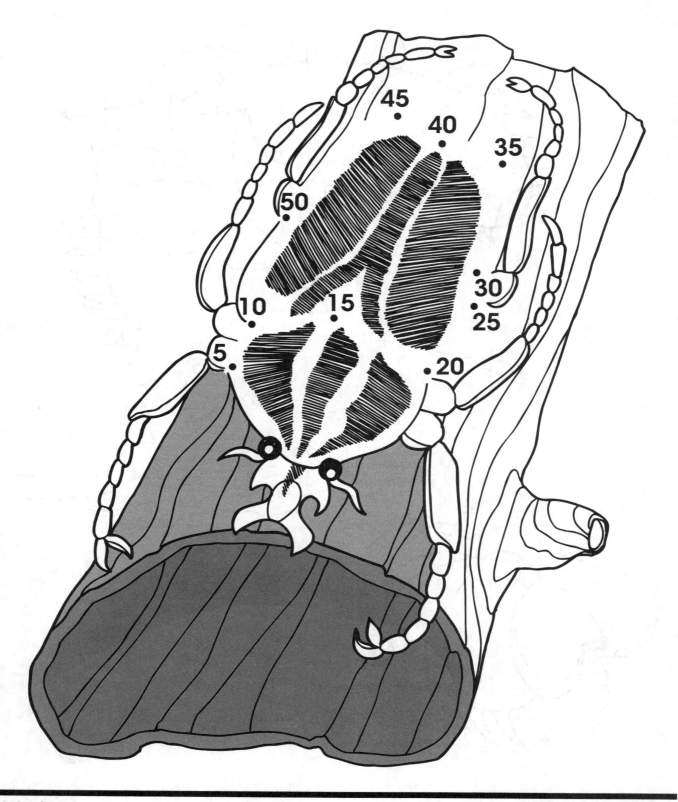

Vera the Velvet Ant

Directions: Connect the dots from **5** to **65**. Then, color to finish the picture.

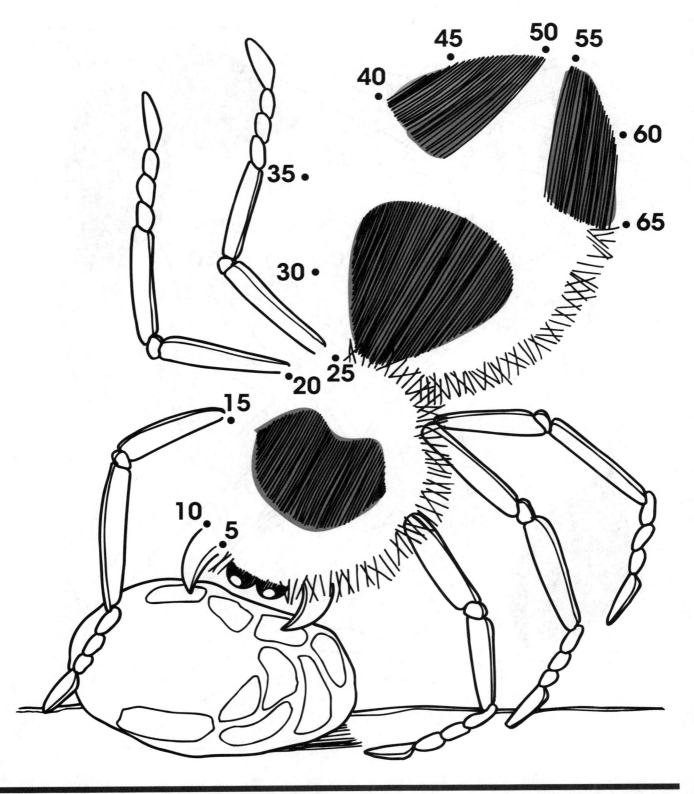

Willy the Walkingstick

Directions: Connect the dots from **0** to **50**. Then, color to finish the picture.

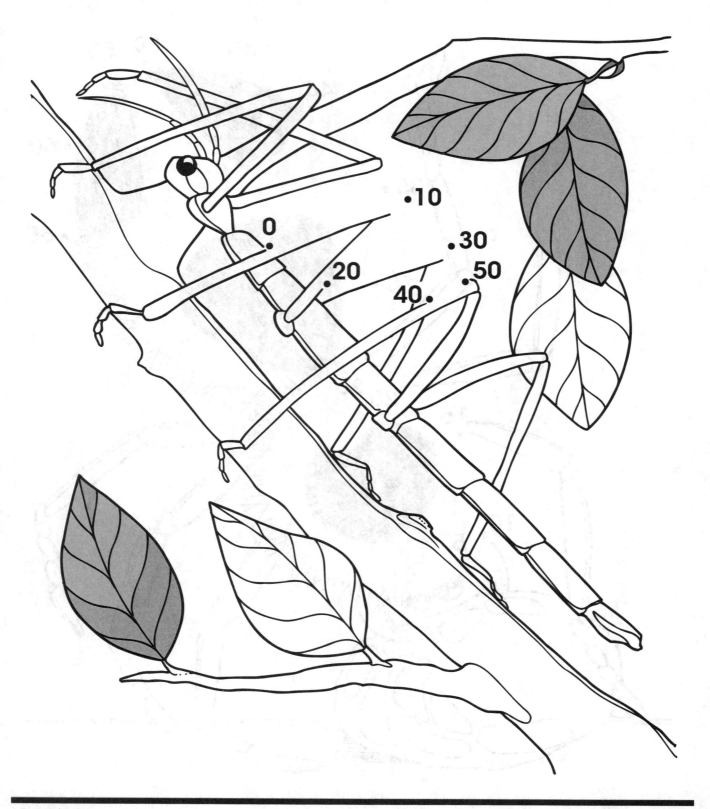

Amy the Atlas Moth

Directions: Connect the dots from **0** to **60**. Then, color to finish the picture.

Walter the Water Bug

Directions: Connect the dots from **0** to **70**. Then, color to finish the picture.

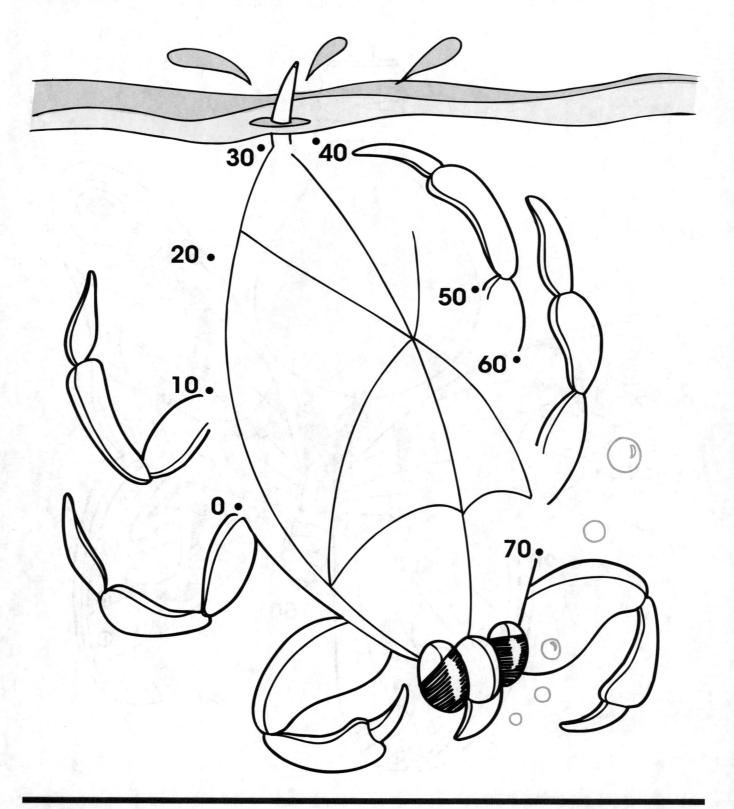

Marty the Mantis

Directions: Connect the dots from **10** to **80**. Then, color to finish the picture.

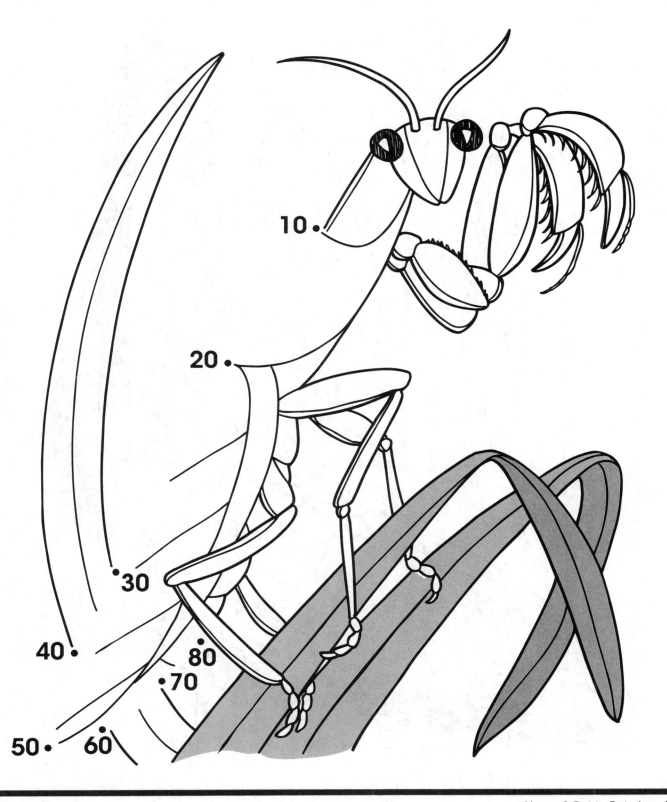

Oscar the Owlet Moth

Directions: Connect the dots from **0** to **90**. Then, color to finish the picture.

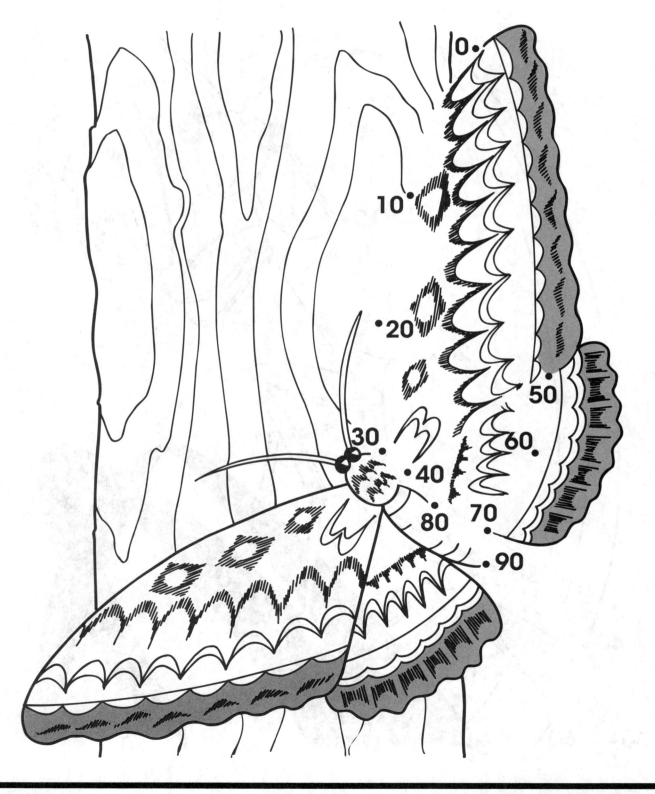

Lily the Ladybug

Directions: Connect the dots from **10** to **100**. Then, color to finish the picture.

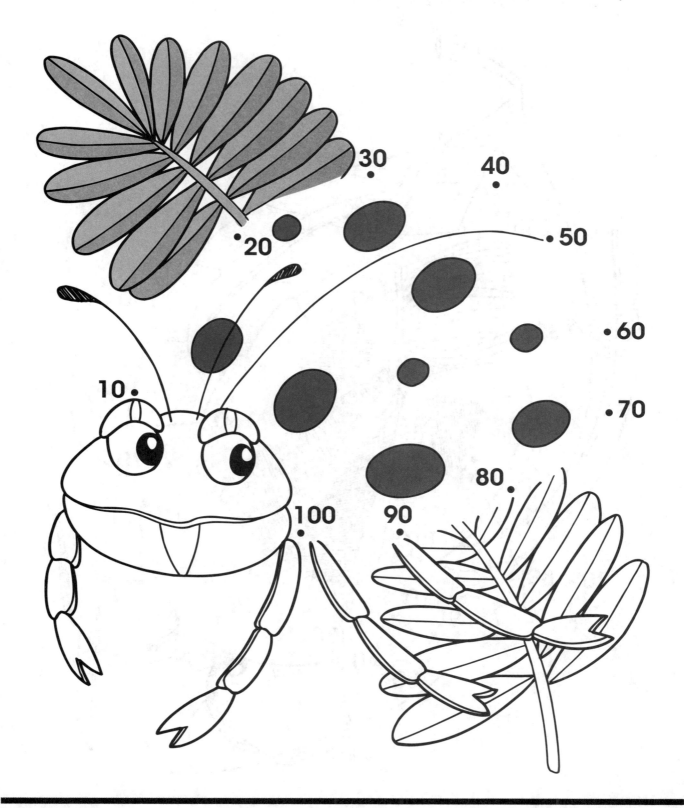

Barry the Beetle

Directions: Connect the dots from **10** to **200**. Then, color to finish the picture.

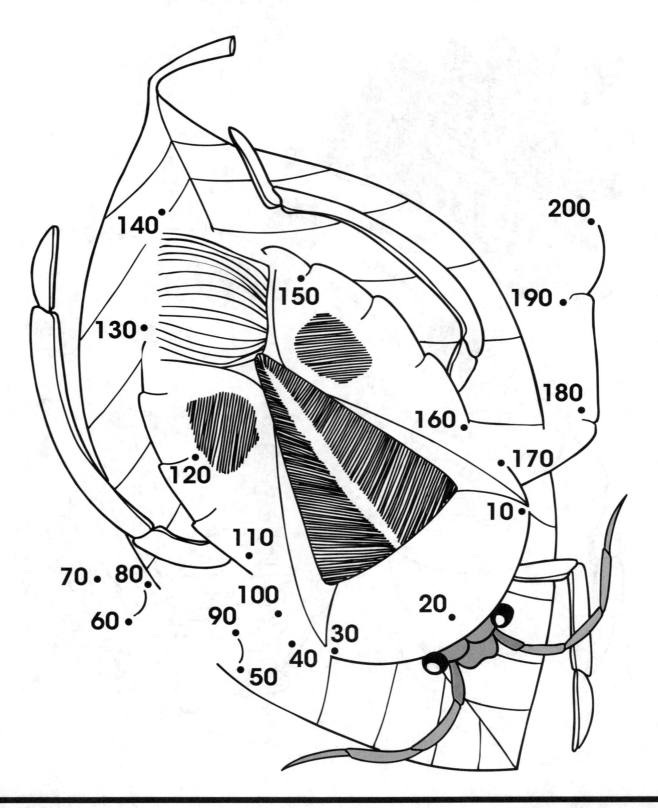

Violet the Violin Beetle

Directions: Connect the dots from **10** to **75**. Then, color to finish the picture.

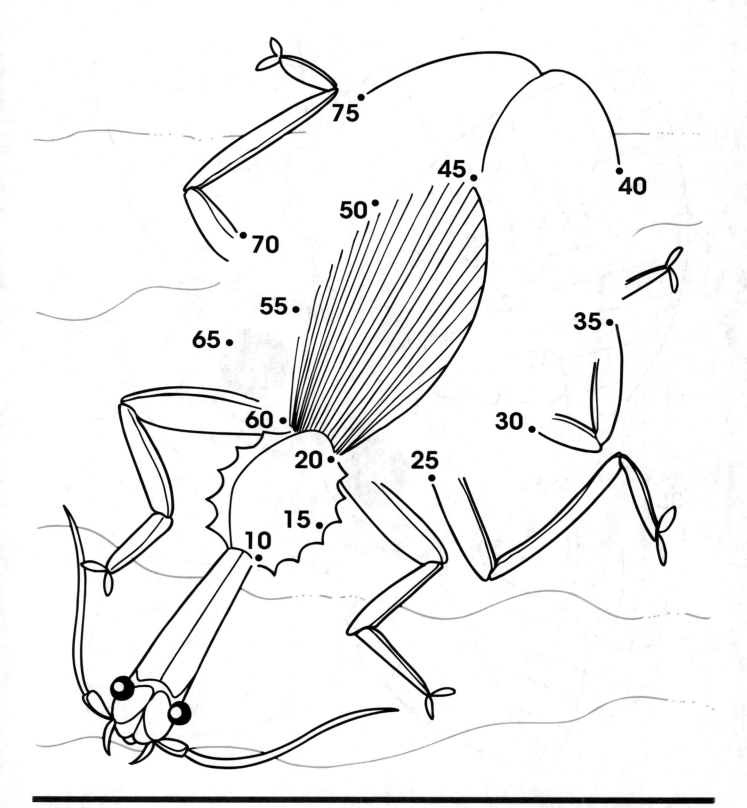

Irene the Io Moth

Directions: Connect the dots from **25** to **100**. Then, color to finish the picture.

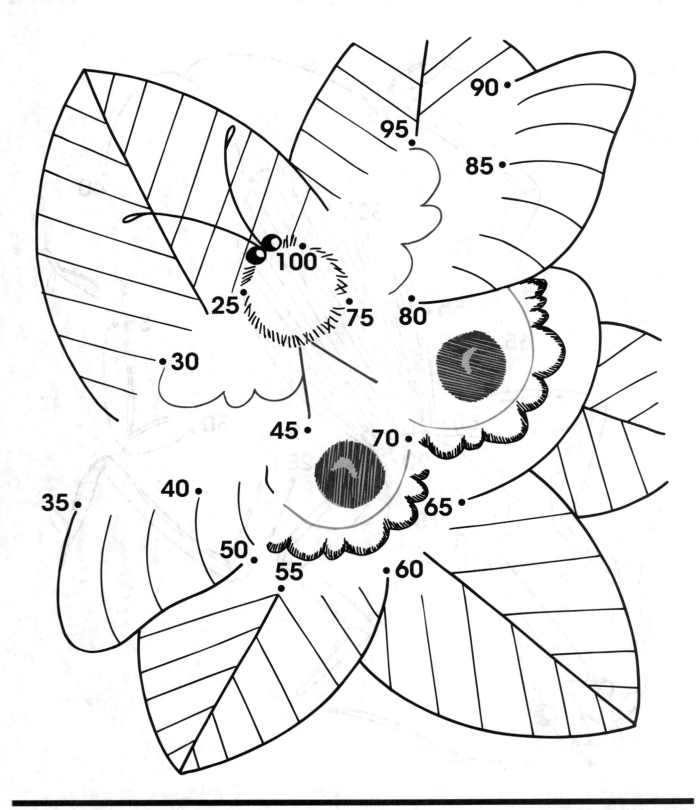

Helen the Housefly

Directions: Connect the dots from **0** to **100**. Then, color to finish the picture.

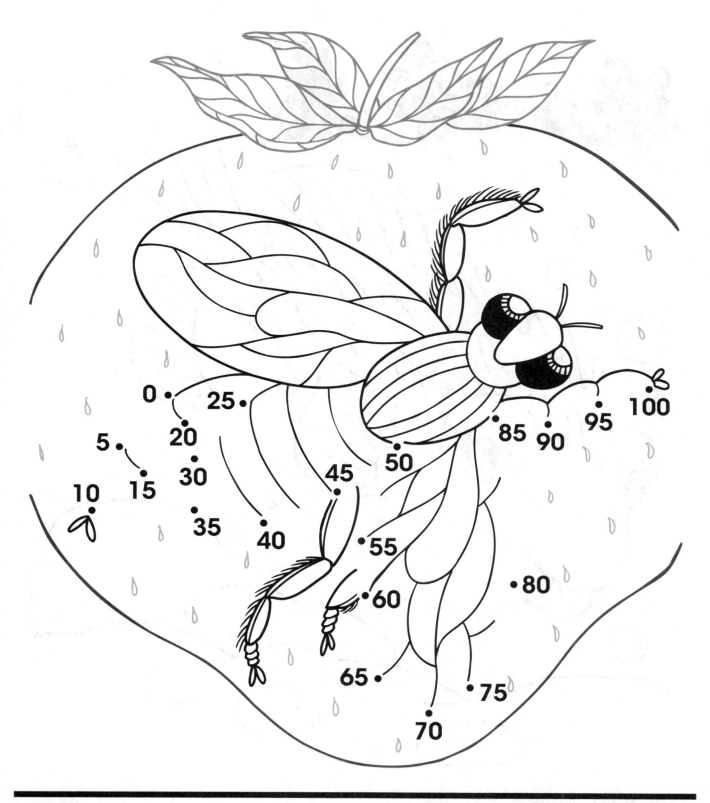

A Pointy Fish

Directions: Connect the dots from **0** to **10**. Then, color to finish the picture.

Fancy Fish

Directions: Connect the dots from **2** to **16**. Then, color to finish the picture.

A Friendly Sea Lion

Directions: Connect the dots from **2** to **20**. Then, color to finish the picture.

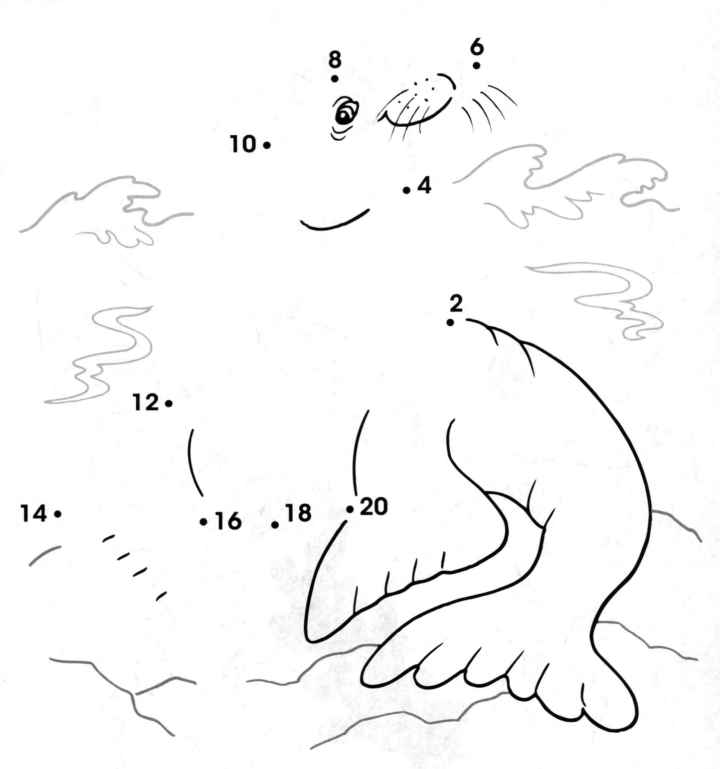

Soldier of the Sea

Directions: Connect the dots from **10** to **28**. Then, color to finish the picture.

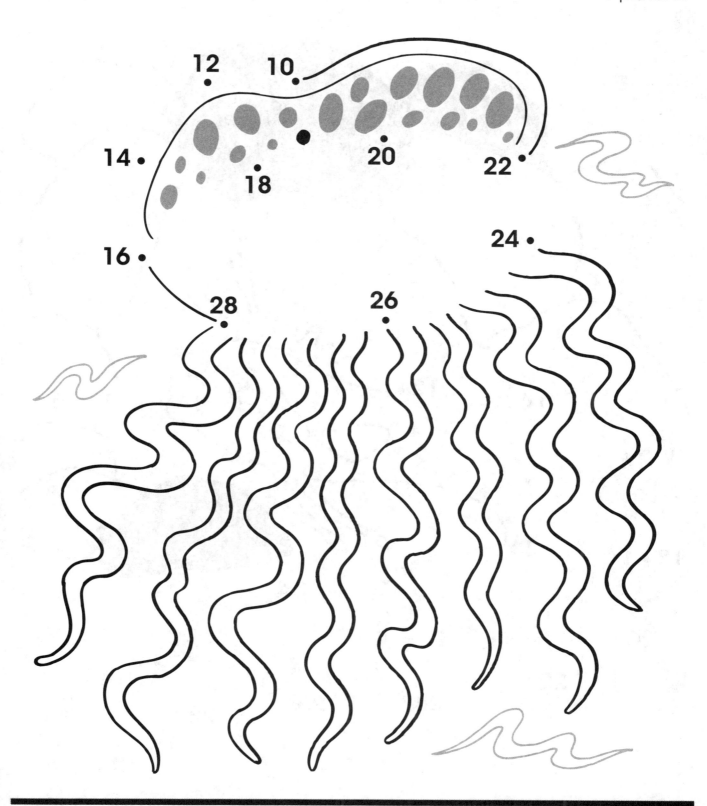

A Long Fish

Directions: Connect the dots from **12** to **38**. Then, color to finish the picture.

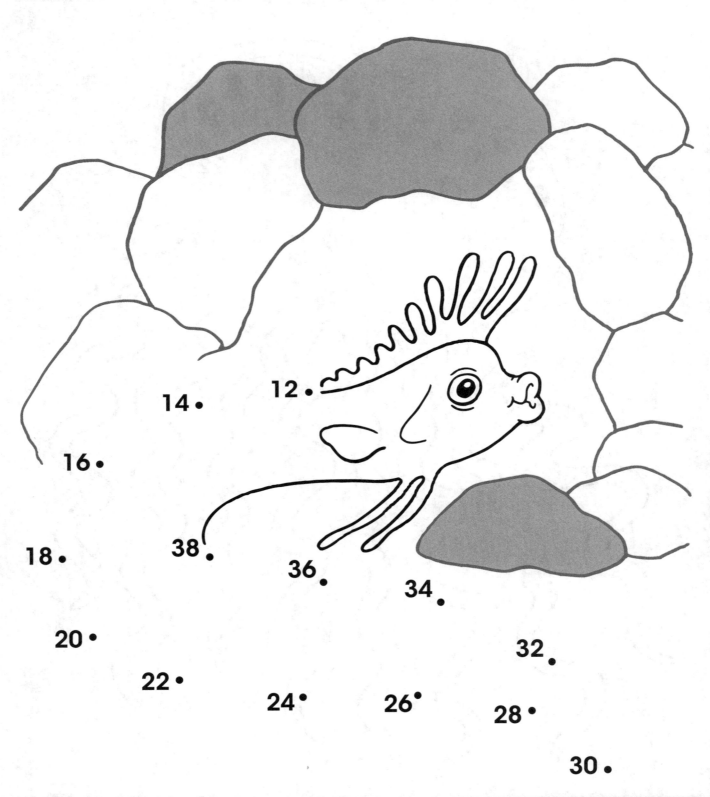

A Big Walrus

Directions: Connect the dots from **15** to **43**. Then, color to finish the picture.

A Tiger Shell?

Directions: Connect the dots from **26** to **60**. Then, color to finish the picture.

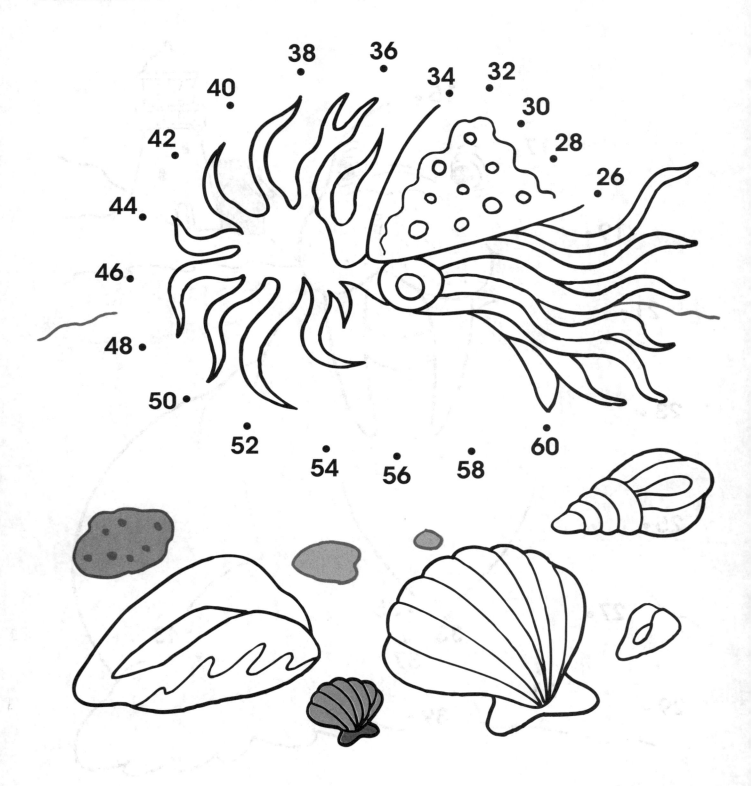

Swim On!

Directions: Connect the dots from **0** to **15**. Then, color to finish the picture.

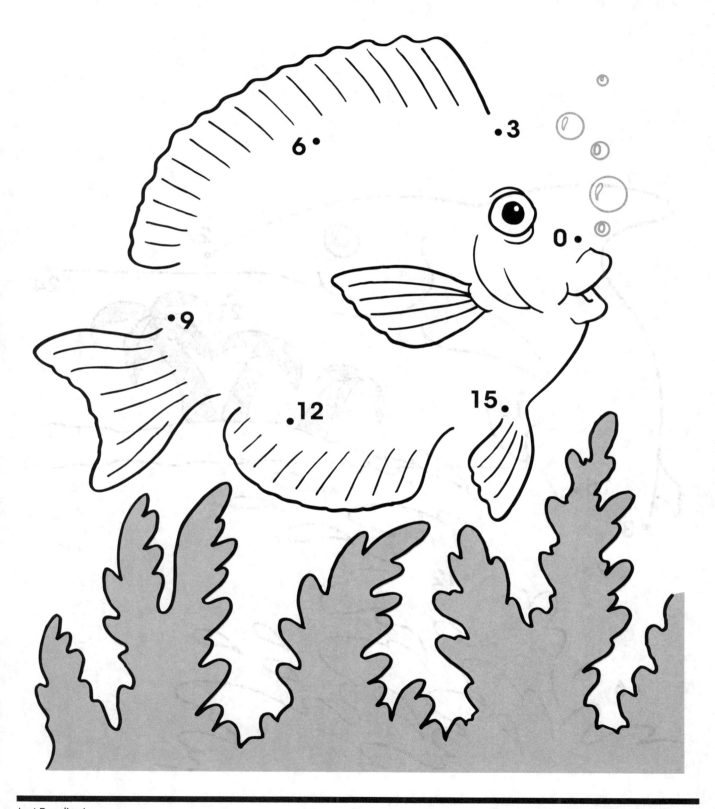

Sharpy Swordfish

Directions: Connect the dots from **3** to **27**. Then, color to finish the picture.

On the Sea Floor

Directions: Connect the dots from **0** to **33**. Then, color to finish the picture.

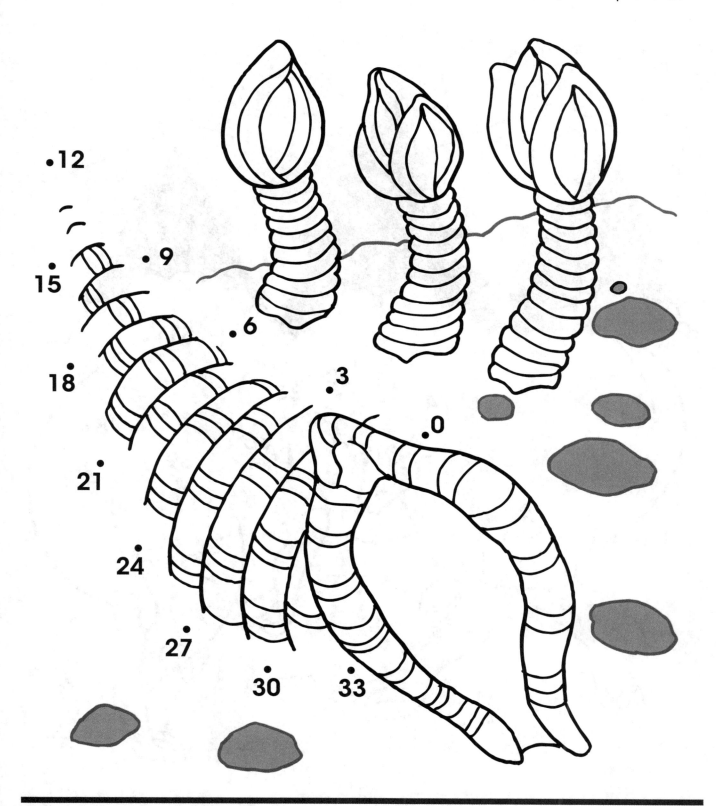

Back in Time

Directions: Connect the dots from **12** to **51**. Then, color to finish the picture.

51

27   30
24   33
•12   36
.15   18   21   39   48
                              42   45

A Smart Coral

Directions: Connect the dots from **9** to **54**. Then, color to finish the picture.

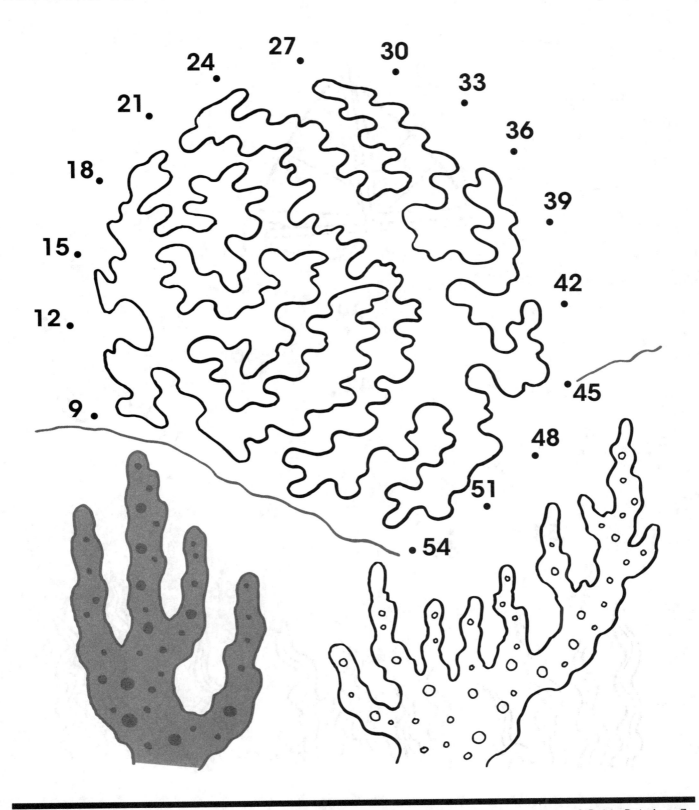

What Shark Is This?

Directions: Connect the dots from **24** to **72**. Then, color to finish the picture.

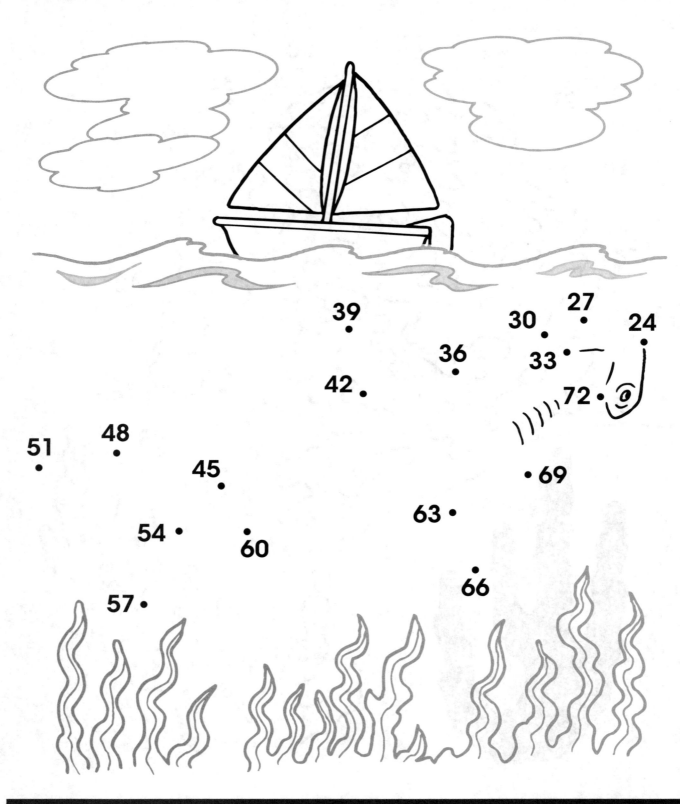

Free to Be Me!

Directions: Connect the dots from **33** to **90**. Then, color to finish the picture.

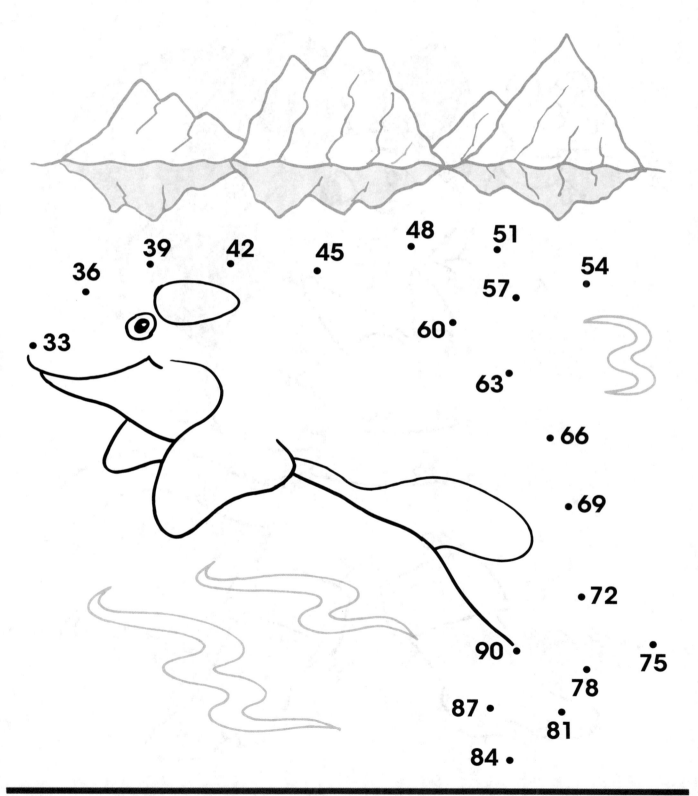

Puss in Boots

Directions: Connect the dots from **0** to **20**. Then, color to finish the picture.

T-rex's Tooth

Directions: Connect the dots from **0** to **24**. Then, color to finish the picture.

Hansel and Gretel

Directions: Connect the dots from **4** to **32**. Then, color to finish the picture.

Duck or a Dino?

Directions: Connect the dots from **4** to **40**. Then, color to finish the picture.

The Emperor's New Clothes

Directions: Connect the dots from **12** to **48**. Then, color to finish the picture.

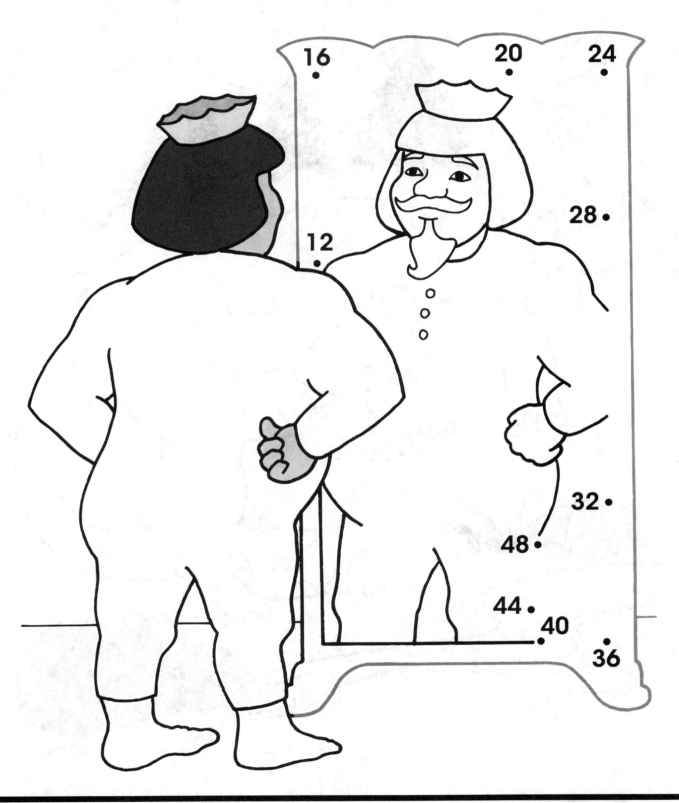

The Three Bears

Directions: Connect the dots from **16** to **68**. Then, color to finish the picture.

Goldilocks

Directions: Connect the dots from **36** to **80**. Then, color to finish the picture.

40

44

48

36 80

76

56 52

72

60

68

64

A Last Dinosaur

Directions: Connect the dots from **28** to **96**. Then, color to finish the picture.

Answer Key

4

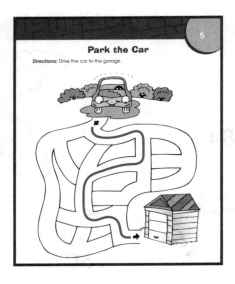

5

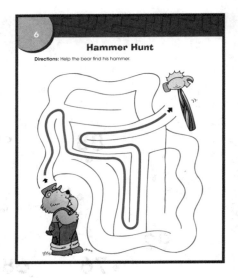

6

7

8

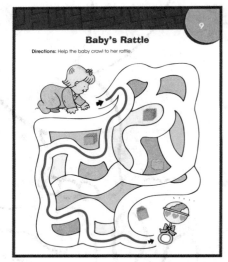

9

Answer Key

A Cold Walk
Directions: Help the penguin find the way to its igloo.

10

Scott's Sled
Directions: Show Scott the trail to his sled.

11

Pete and Peggy Pig
Directions: Will Pete or Peggy get the ice-cream cone?

12

Fishy Friends
Directions: Help the striped fish swim through the coral and find its friend.

13

Field Goal
Directions: Kick the football through the goalposts.

14

All Dry
Directions: The clothes are dry. Help put them in the basket.

15

Answer Key

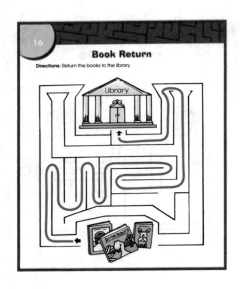

16

17

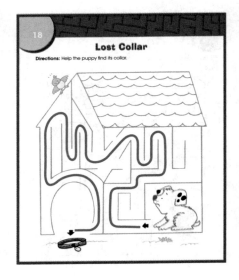

18

19

20

21

Answer Key

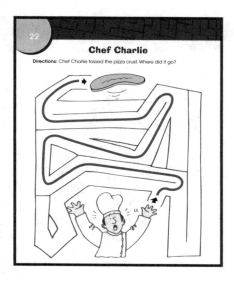

22

23

24

25

26

27

Answer Key

Humpty Dumpty

Directions: Help Humpty Dumpty find the bandage. Then, color the picture.

28

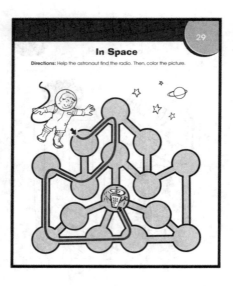

In Space

Directions: Help the astronaut find the radio. Then, color the picture.

29

Where's the Turkey?

Directions: Help the pilgrim boy find the turkey. Then, color the picture.

30

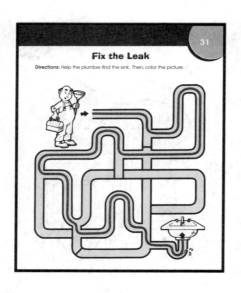

Fix the Leak

Directions: Help the plumber find the sink. Then, color the picture.

31

A Missing Slipper

Directions: Help the ballerina find her slipper. Then, color the picture.

32

A Lost Kangaroo

Directions: Help the mother kangaroo find her baby.

33

Answer Key

34
A Prince and a Princess
Directions: Help the prince get to the princess. Then, color the picture.

34

35
I'm Late
Directions: Help the lady get to the train. Then, color the picture.

35

36
A Perky Penguin
Directions: Help the mother penguin find the baby penguin.

36

37
Lock and Key
Directions: Help the key find the lock.

37

38
Sail Away
Directions: Help the sailor find the anchor.

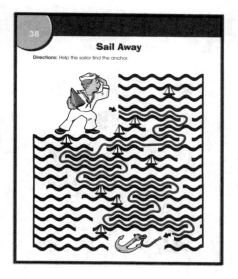

38

39
Dana Deer
Directions: Connect the dots from 1 to 15. Then, color to finish the picture.

39

Answer Key

40

41

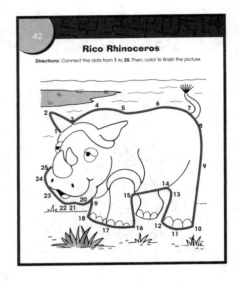

42

43

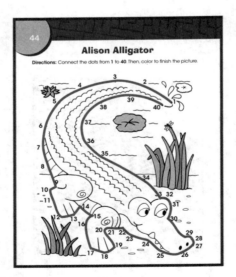

44

45

Answer Key

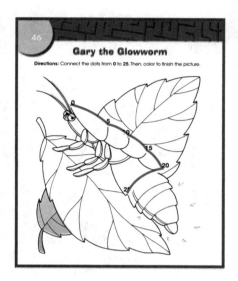

46

47

48

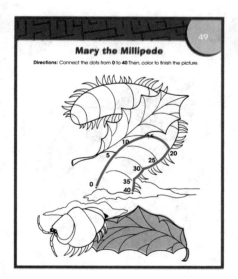

49

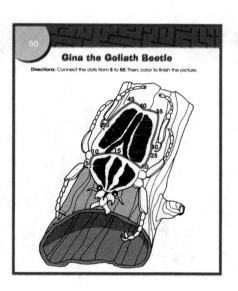

50

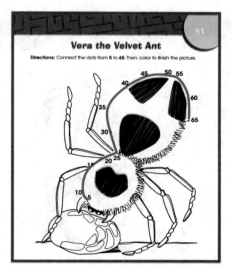

51

Answer Key

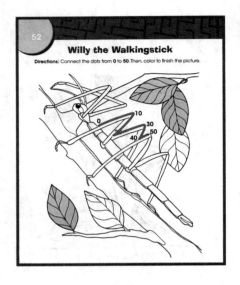

Willy the Walkingstick
Directions: Connect the dots from **0** to **50**. Then, color to finish the picture.

52

Amy the Atlas Moth
Directions: Connect the dots from **0** to **60**. Then, color to finish the picture.

53

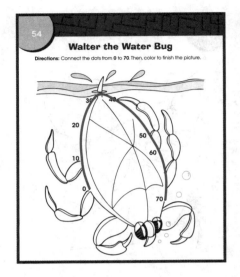

Walter the Water Bug
Directions: Connect the dots from **0** to **70**. Then, color to finish the picture.

54

Marty the Mantis
Directions: Connect the dots from **10** to **80**. Then, color to finish the picture.

55

Oscar the Owlet Moth
Directions: Connect the dots from **0** to **90**. Then, color to finish the picture.

56

Lily the Ladybug
Directions: Connect the dots from **10** to **100**. Then, color to finish the picture.

57

Answer Key

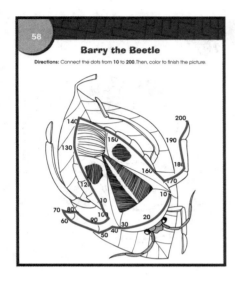

58

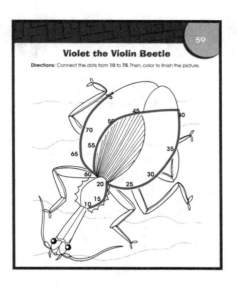

59

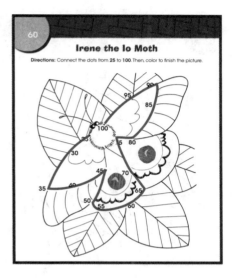

60

61

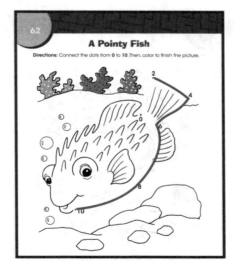

62

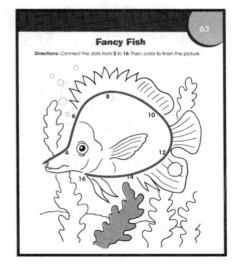

63

Answer Key

64

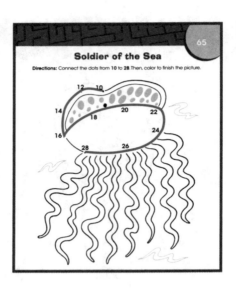

65

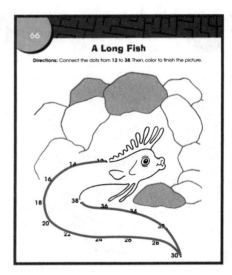

66

67

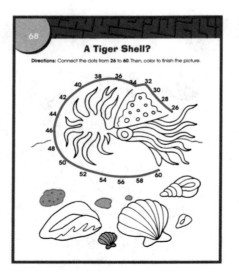

68

69

Answer Key

Sharpy Swordfish
Directions: Connect the dots from **3** to **27**. Then, color to finish the picture.

70

On the Sea Floor
Directions: Connect the dots from **0** to **33**. Then, color to finish the picture.

71

Back in Time
Directions: Connect the dots from **12** to **51**. Then, color to finish the picture.

72

A Smart Coral
Directions: Connect the dots from **9** to **54**. Then, color to finish the picture.

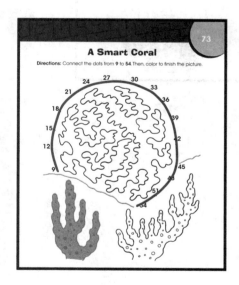

73

What Shark Is This?
Directions: Connect the dots from **24** to **72**. Then, color to finish the picture.

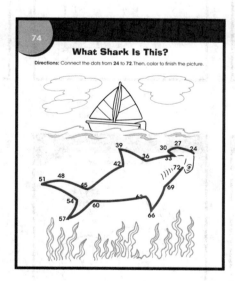

74

Free to Be Me!
Directions: Connect the dots from **33** to **90**. Then, color to finish the picture.

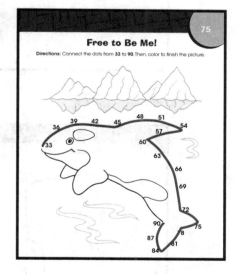

75

Answer Key

76

77

78

79

80

81

82

83